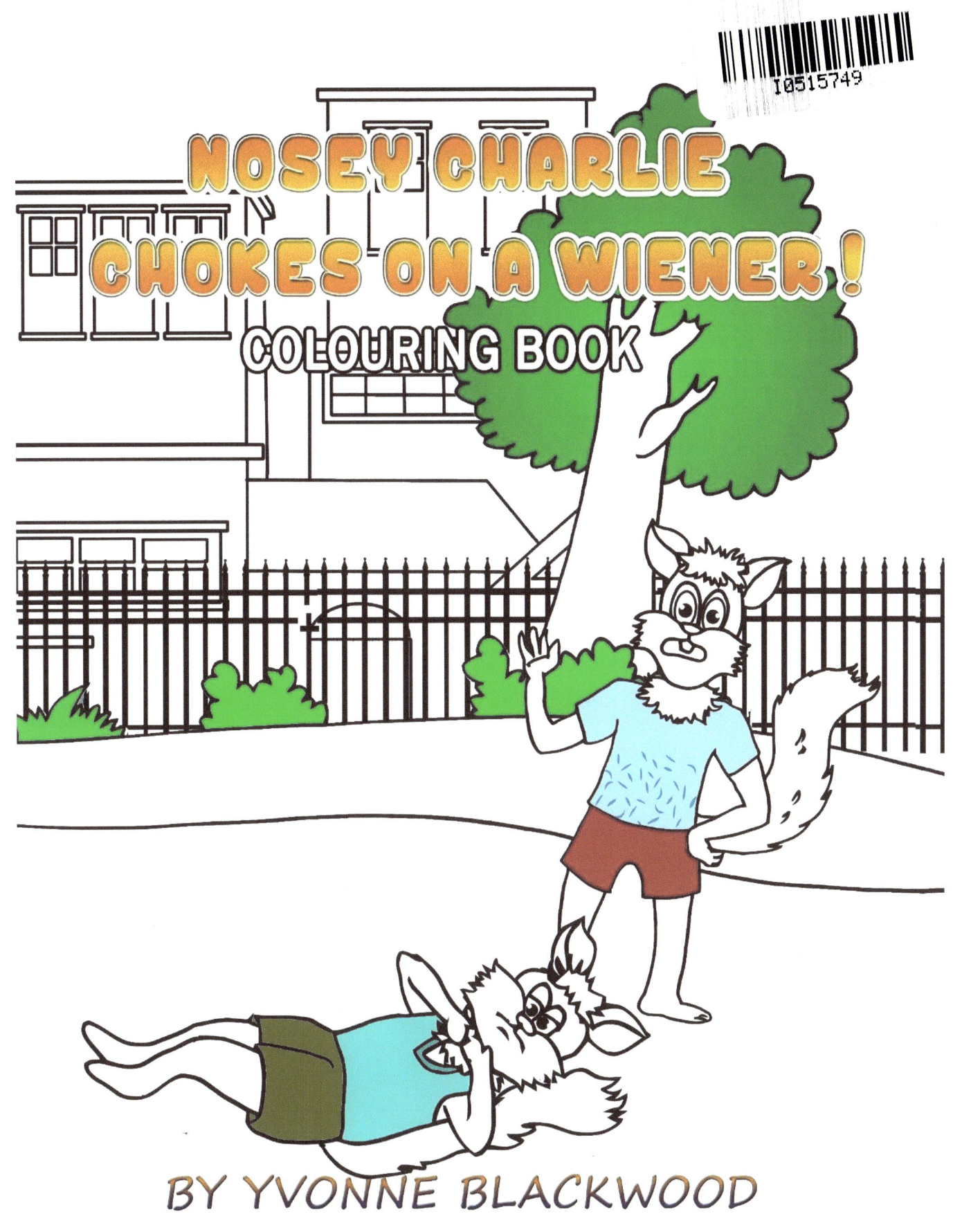

NOSEY CHARLIE CHOKES ON A WIENER!
COLOURING BOOK

BY

YVONNE BLACKWOOD

Illustrated by Artsam

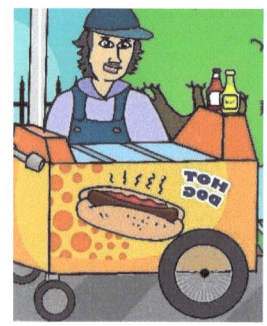

Copyright © 2017 by Yvonne Blackwood

All rights reserved. No part of this book may be reproduced, transmitted, or stored in an information retrieval system in any form or by any means, graphic, electronic, or mechanical, including photocopying, taping, and recording, without prior written permission from Quilloration Enterprise.

First edition 2017

Quilloration Enterprise

Toronto, Ontario

For my grandsons, Theo and Anthony, and all the young

Charlieites.

Unleash your creativity and colour with imagination.

Y.B

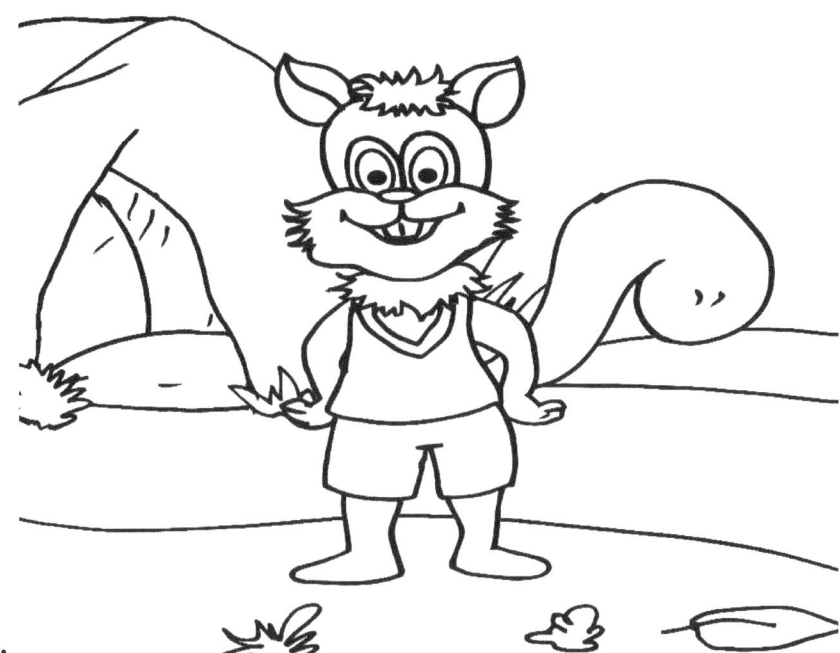

This is Charlie.

He once lived in the country with his mother and father.

When he became an orphan he moved to the city to live with his uncle and aunt, and his cousin Pete Berryhill. That was when Pete's troubles started.

Charlie was a good little squirrel, but he was very nosey.

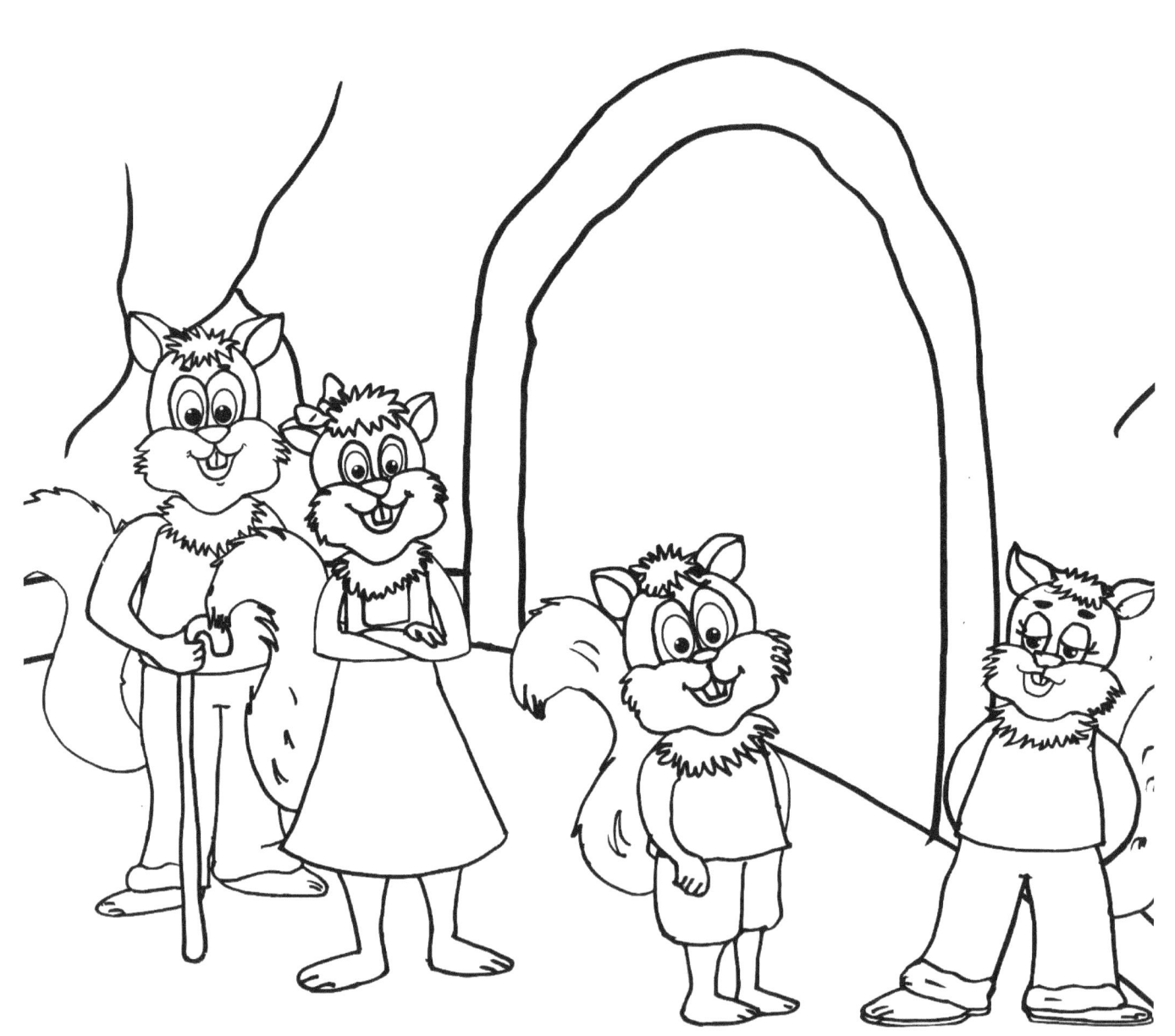

It was Charlie's first summer living in the big city at Courtyard Park and he wanted to see everything. Charlie dashed out of the den as if he was on an emergency call.

"Charlie, wait! I need to speak to you," Mama Berryhill called after him. He didn't wait for Mama Berryhill's instructions, and that was a pity, for he knew so little about the big city.

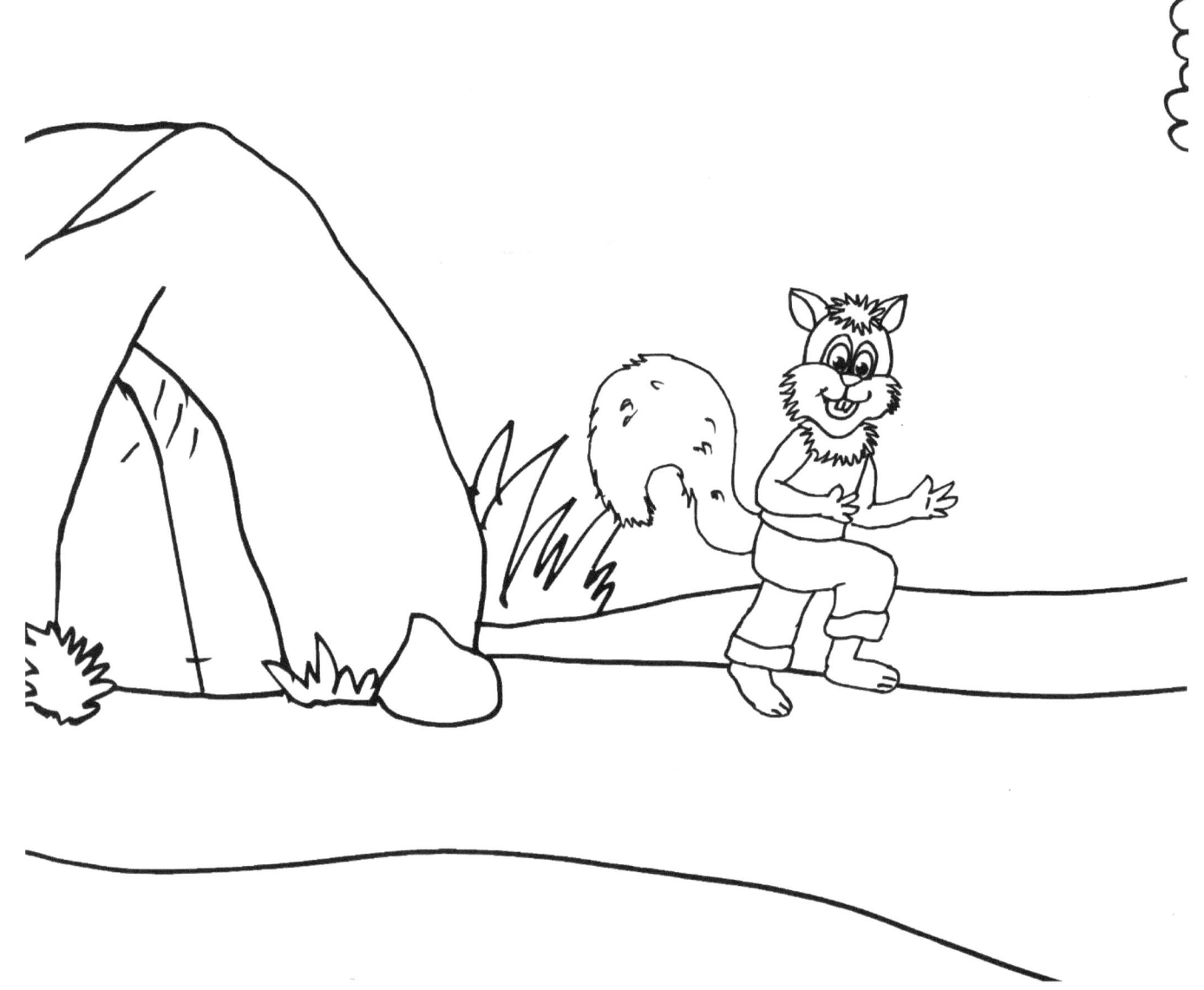

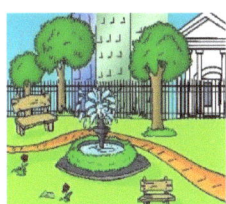

As Charlie roamed about the park he smelled the delicious aroma of hotdogs cooking on a grill. He peered through the tall iron fence that surrounded the park. He saw a hot dog vendor who had parked his cart on the sidewalk. A red umbrella shaded the cart, but Charlie could see the man grilling wieners and toasting buns. Charlie went closer.

"Mmmmm, it smells so GOOOOOOD!" Charlie said.

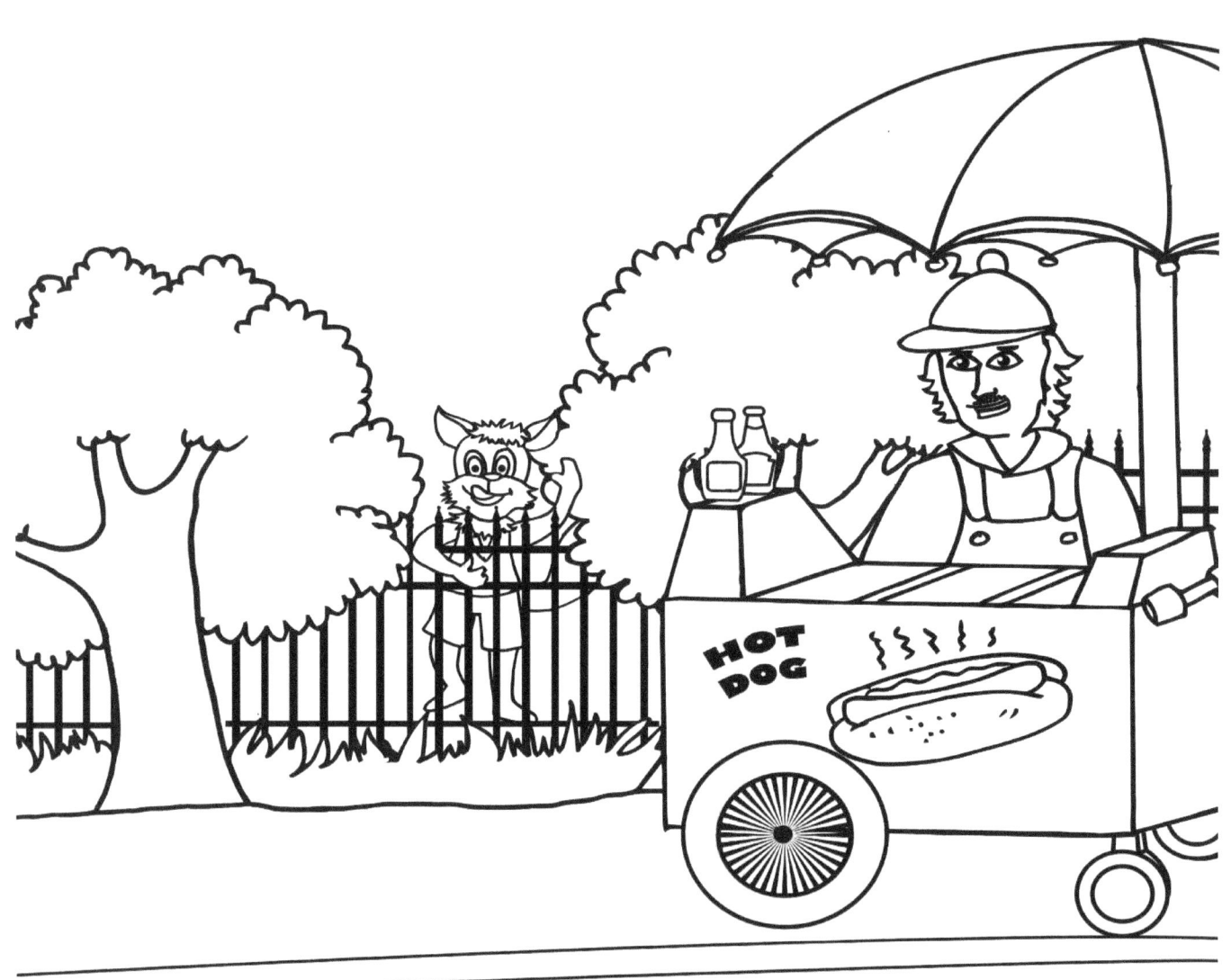

A lot of people walked by—men dressed in suits with bright neckties, women in white skirts and colourful tops, eating French fries. A group of men dressed in black robes that bellowed in the wind walked briskly by. He wondered if they would take off and fly!

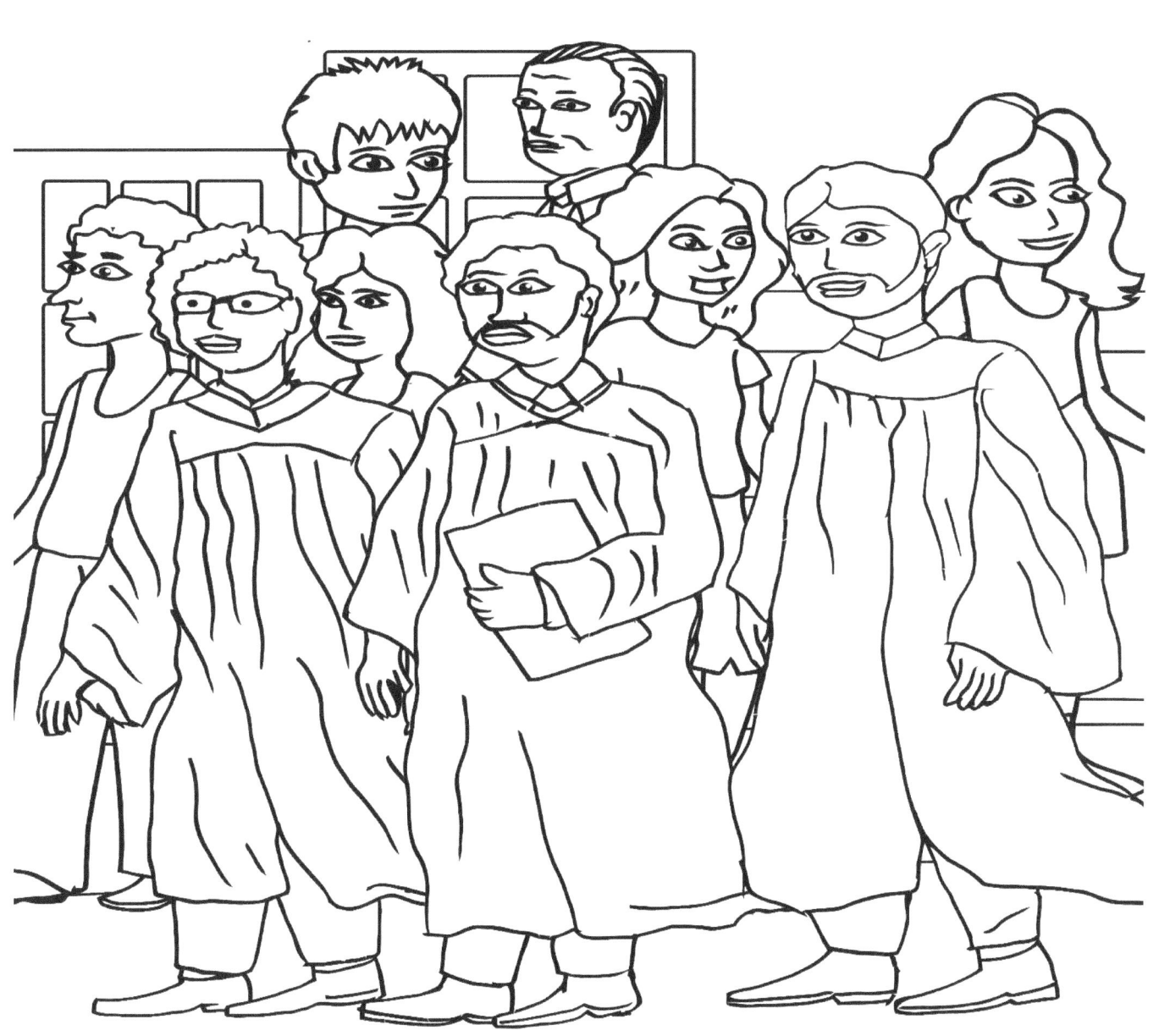

Back at the den, Mama Berryhill said, "Pete, please go find Charlie and watch him like a brother. Remember he's not a city squirrel like us. He's from the country far away, a place with few people, no traffic, and no skyscrapers. To him, everything here is new and strange, and exciting. We don't want your cousin getting into any trouble."

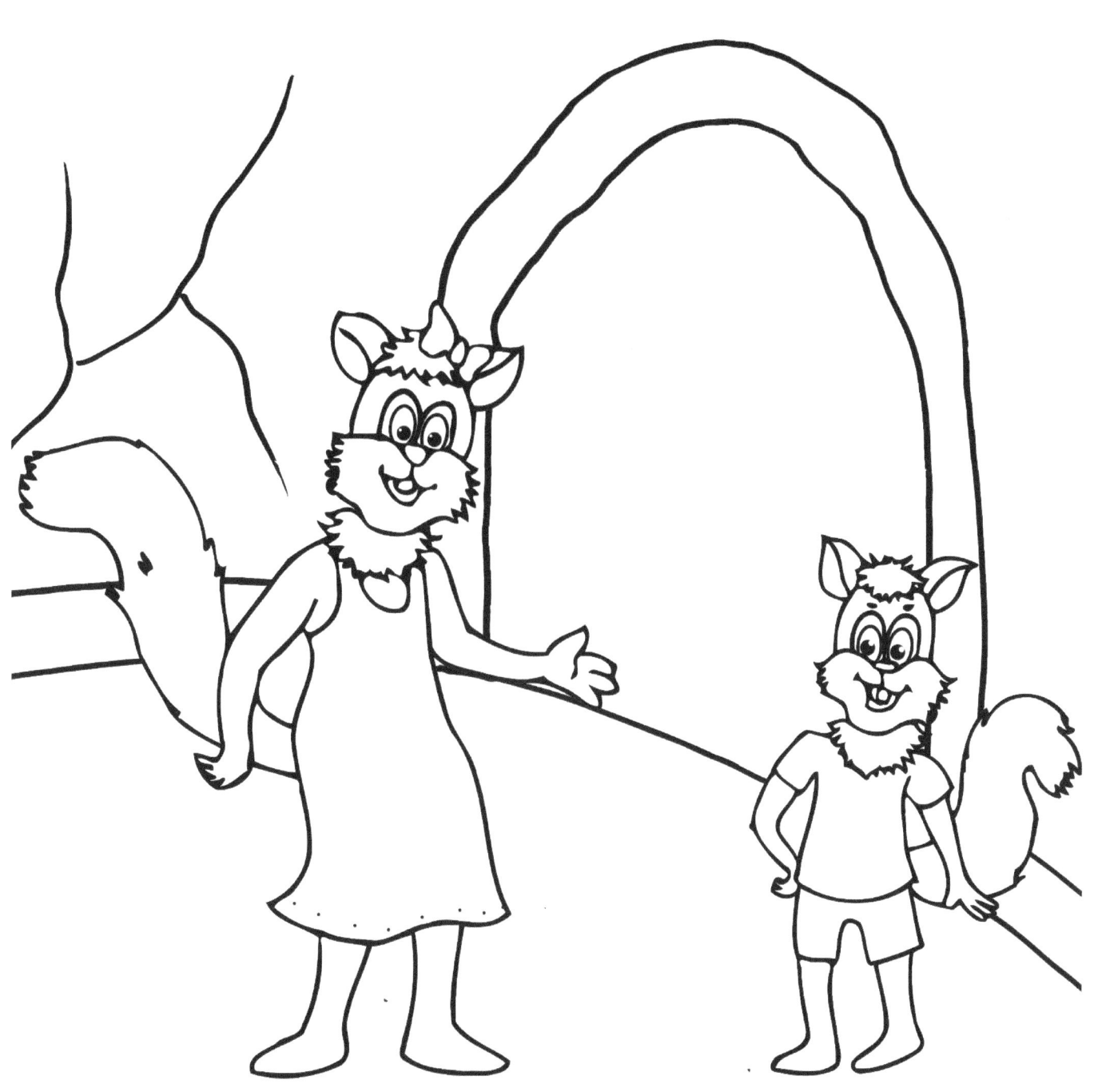

Pete pouted and didn't budge.

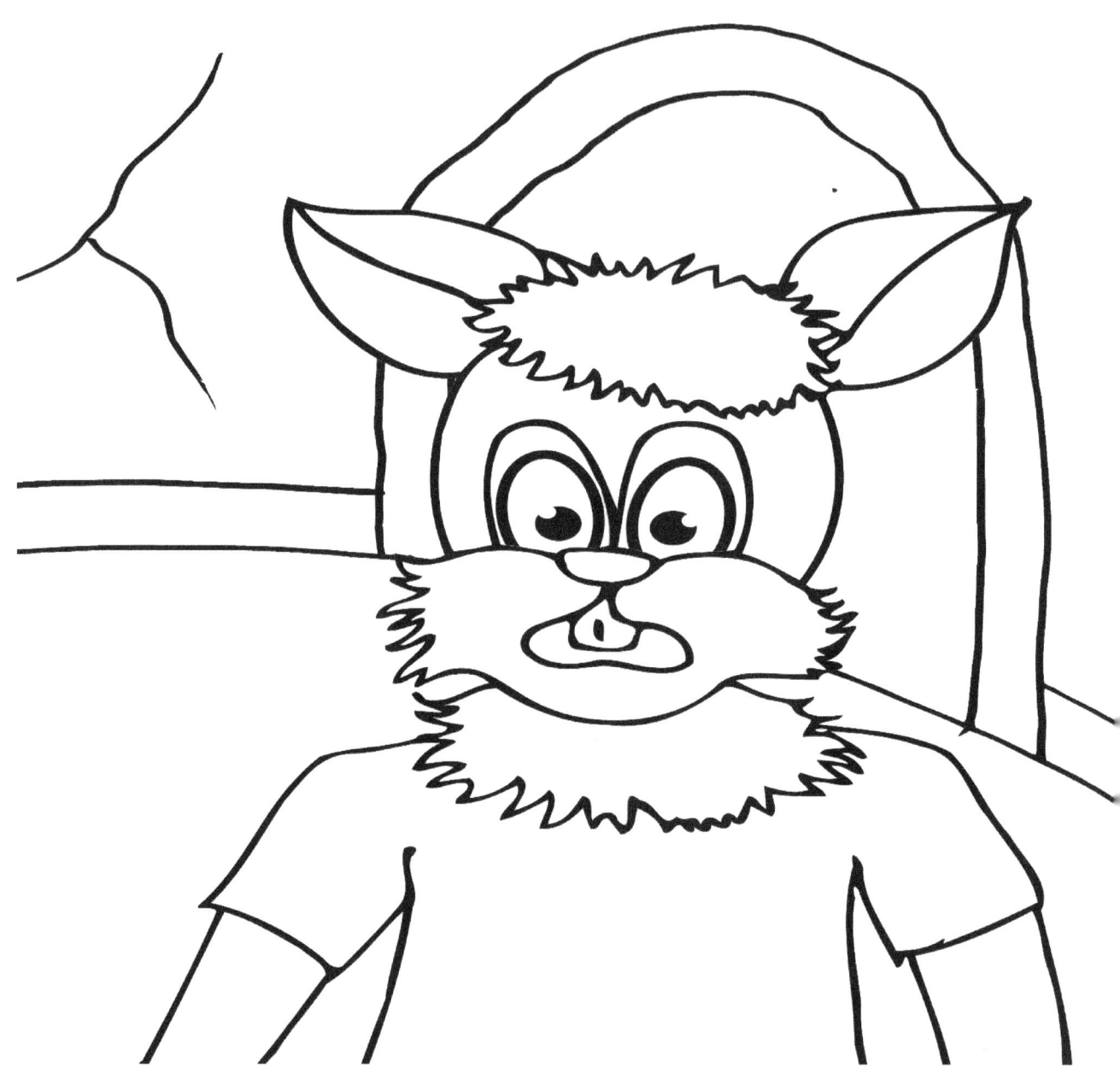

Mama Berryhill crossed her arms and yelled, "On the double!"

Pete went out and searched the park for a short time, but he was not keen to look for his cousin.

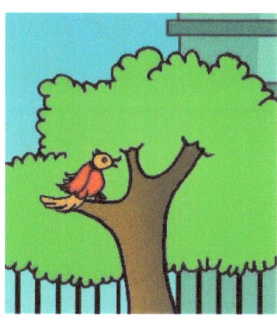

He felt the hot summer sun soaking into his skin. He looked at the smooth grass that had just been mowed. He wanted to lie in it and roll over and over like a football. He looked at the trees covered in leaves. Flocks of birds darted from branch to branch, chirping sweet songs.

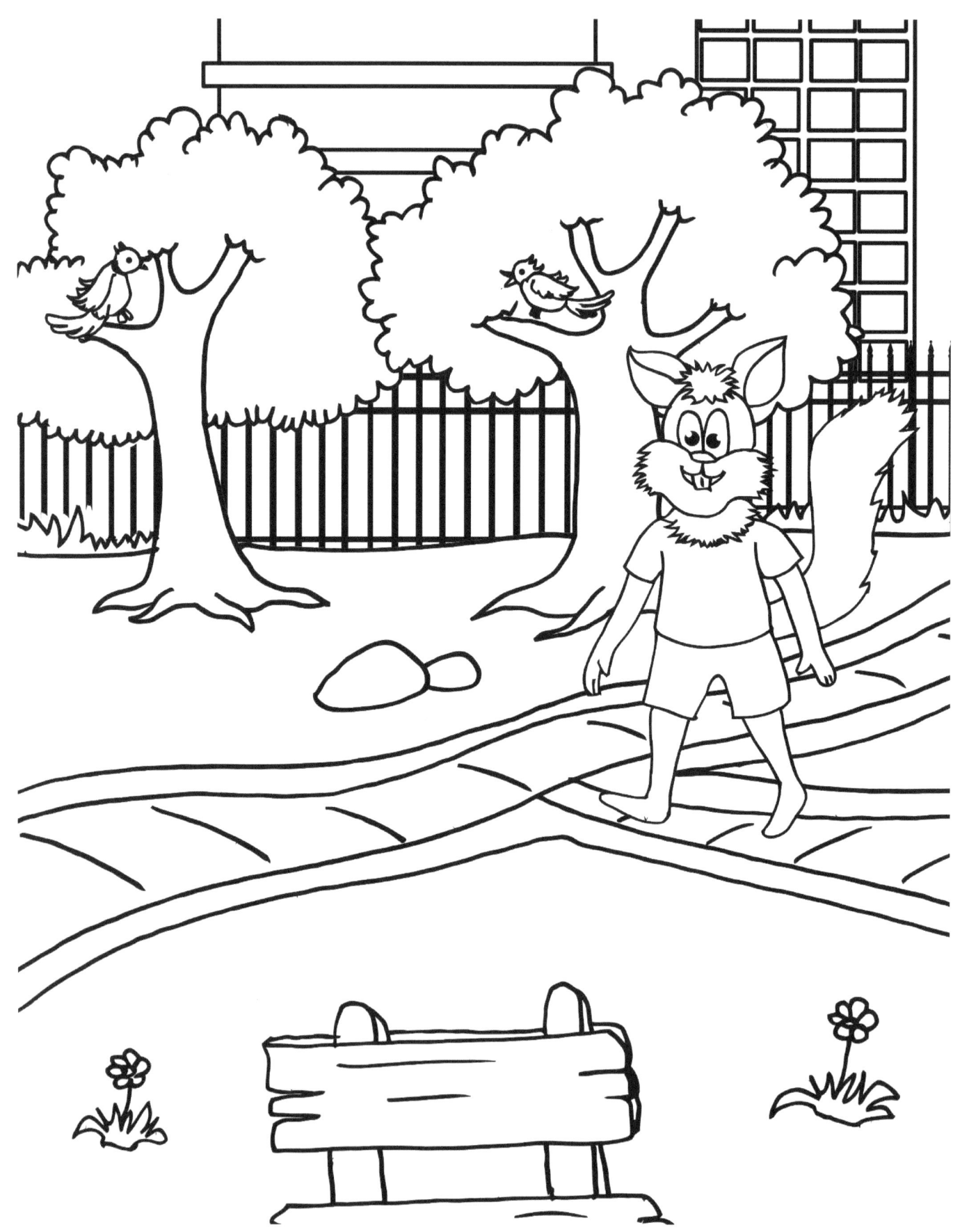

Pete walked to the far side of the park and sat on a bench. He gazed at a waterfall with the water cascading over rocks and running down. Everything was so beautiful in Courtyard Park. As Pete admired the place that had been his home since he was born, he forgot what Mama Berryhill said.

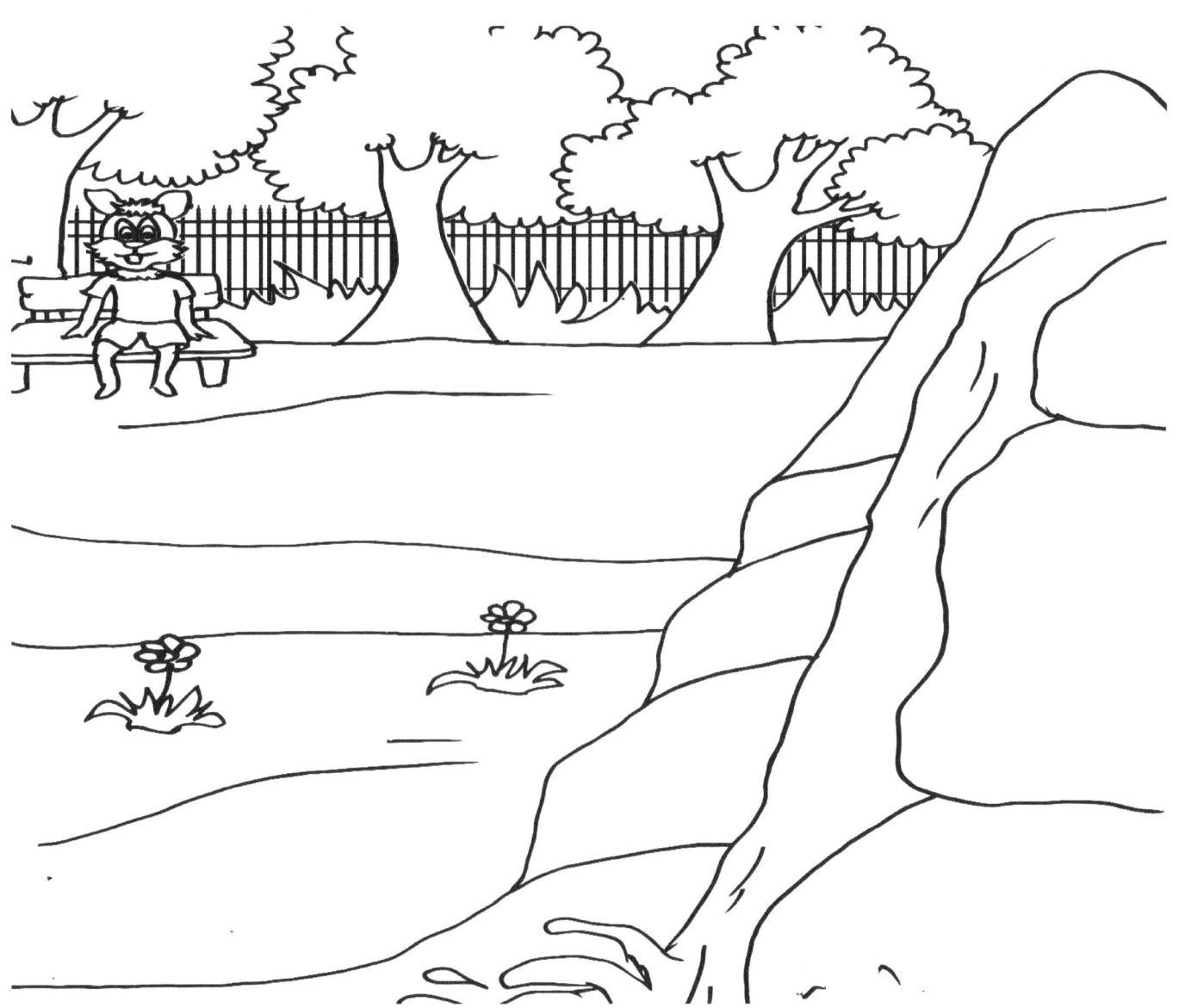

Suddenly, a woman screamed, "Help! P-L-E-A-S-E help the poor animal!"

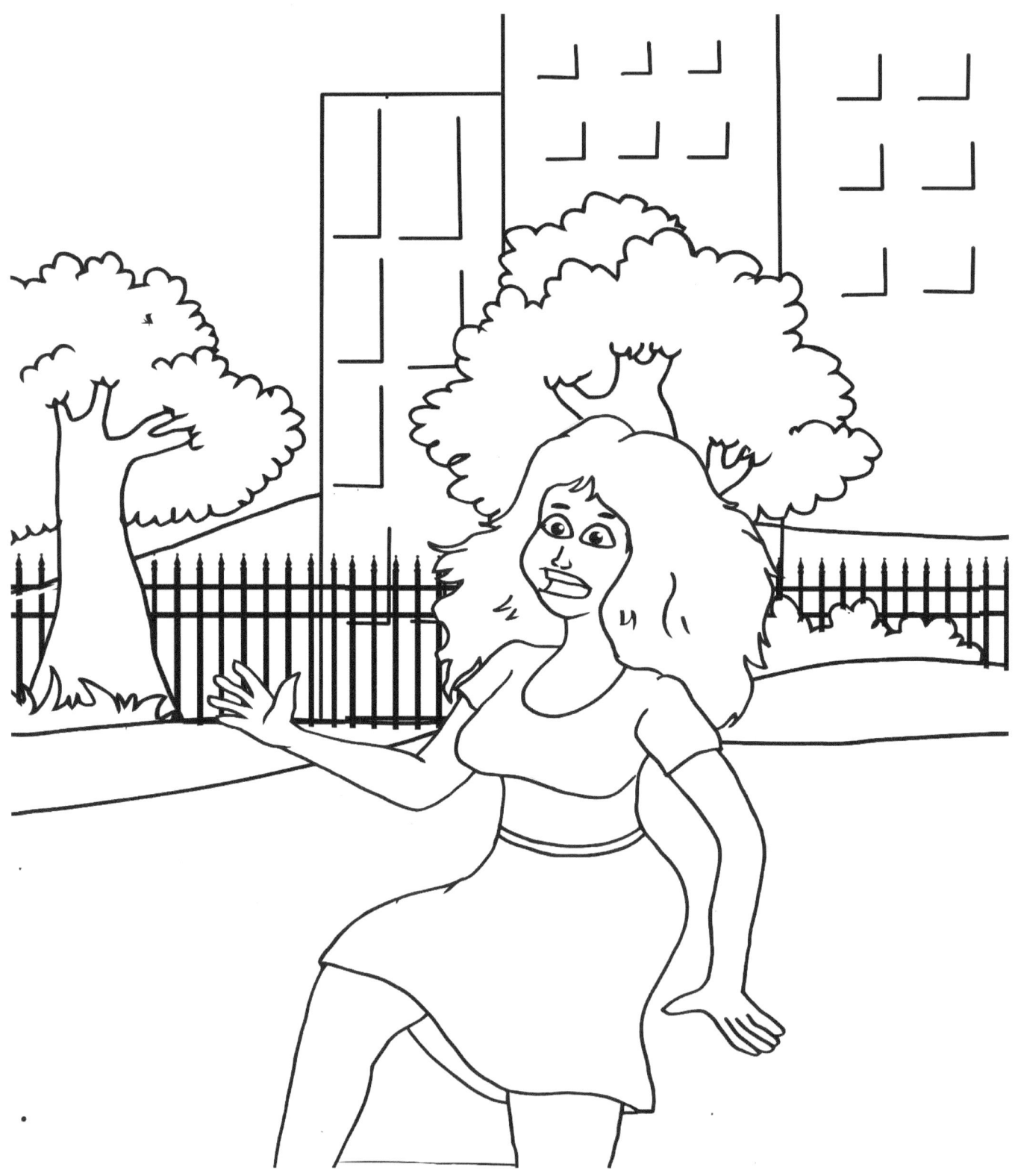

Pete sprang from the bench and dashed toward the direction of the scream to see what caused the commotion. He caught his breath when he saw Charlie in contortion, gasping and gulping, and trying to get air. He was rolling on the grass with his eyes about to pop out of his head.

"Charlie, what is the matter? Charlie, speak to me!" Pete said.

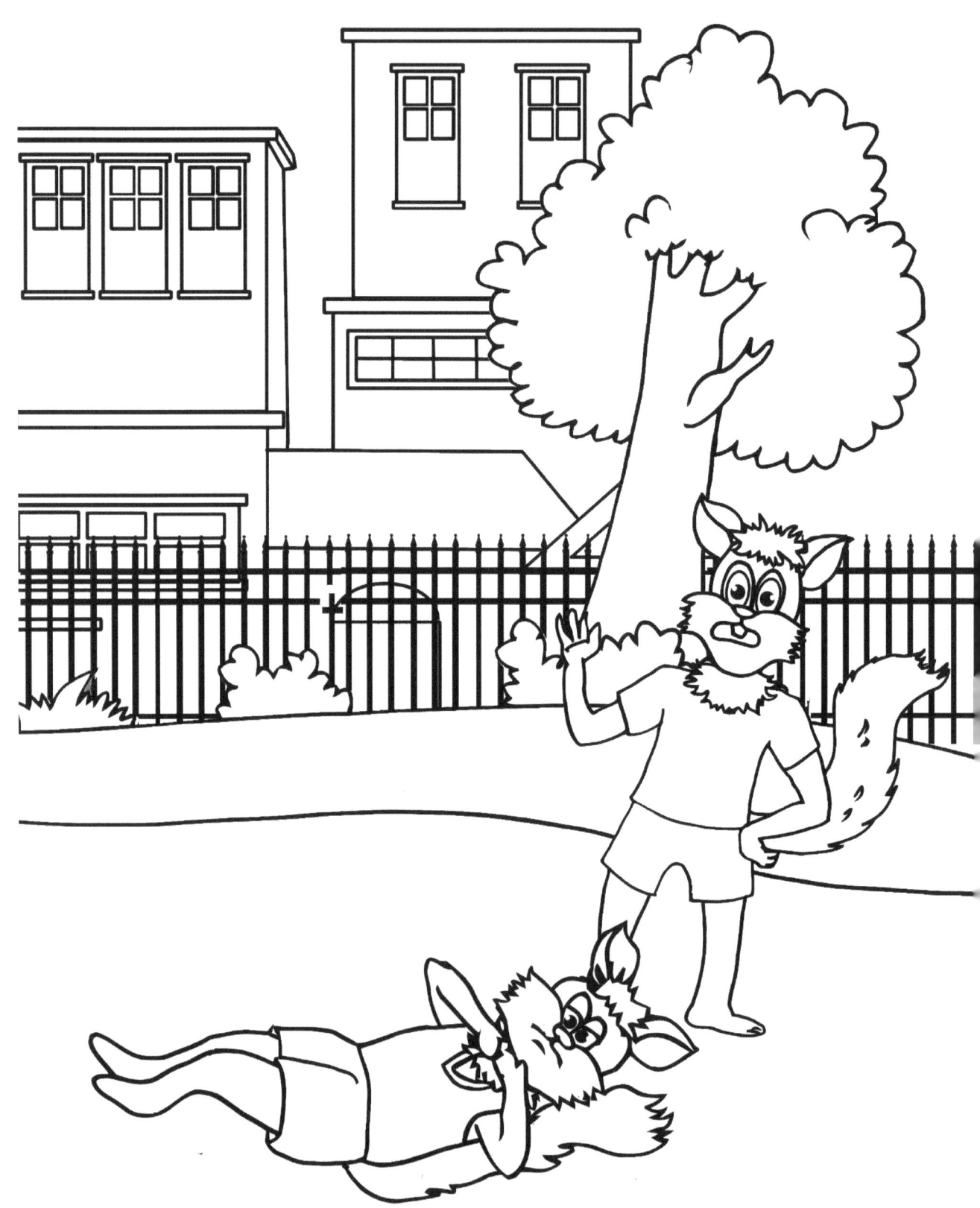

But Charlie did not reply. Something was stuck in his throat. Pete saw a large lump there and winced. What was it? How did it get there?

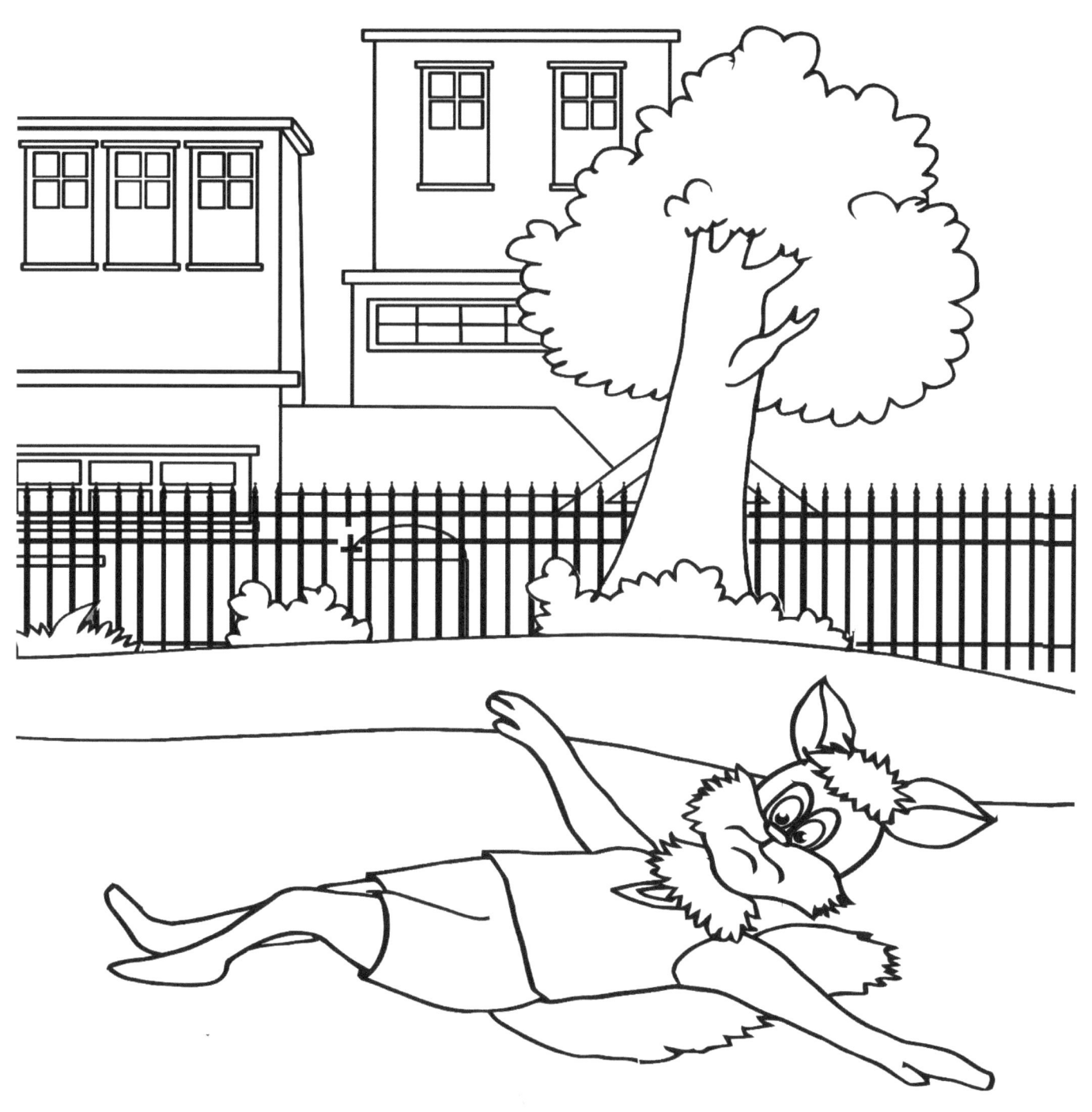

A crowd gathered on the sidewalk at the other side of the fence near the hot dog stand. They were worried, concerned and tense. One man shouted at the hot dog vendor, "You silly birdbrain, why did you feed the squirrel that wiener? They eat nuts, seeds, and berries, not meat, you nitwit. Now the poor creature may die. YOU'LL BE RESPONSIBLE FOR THAT!"

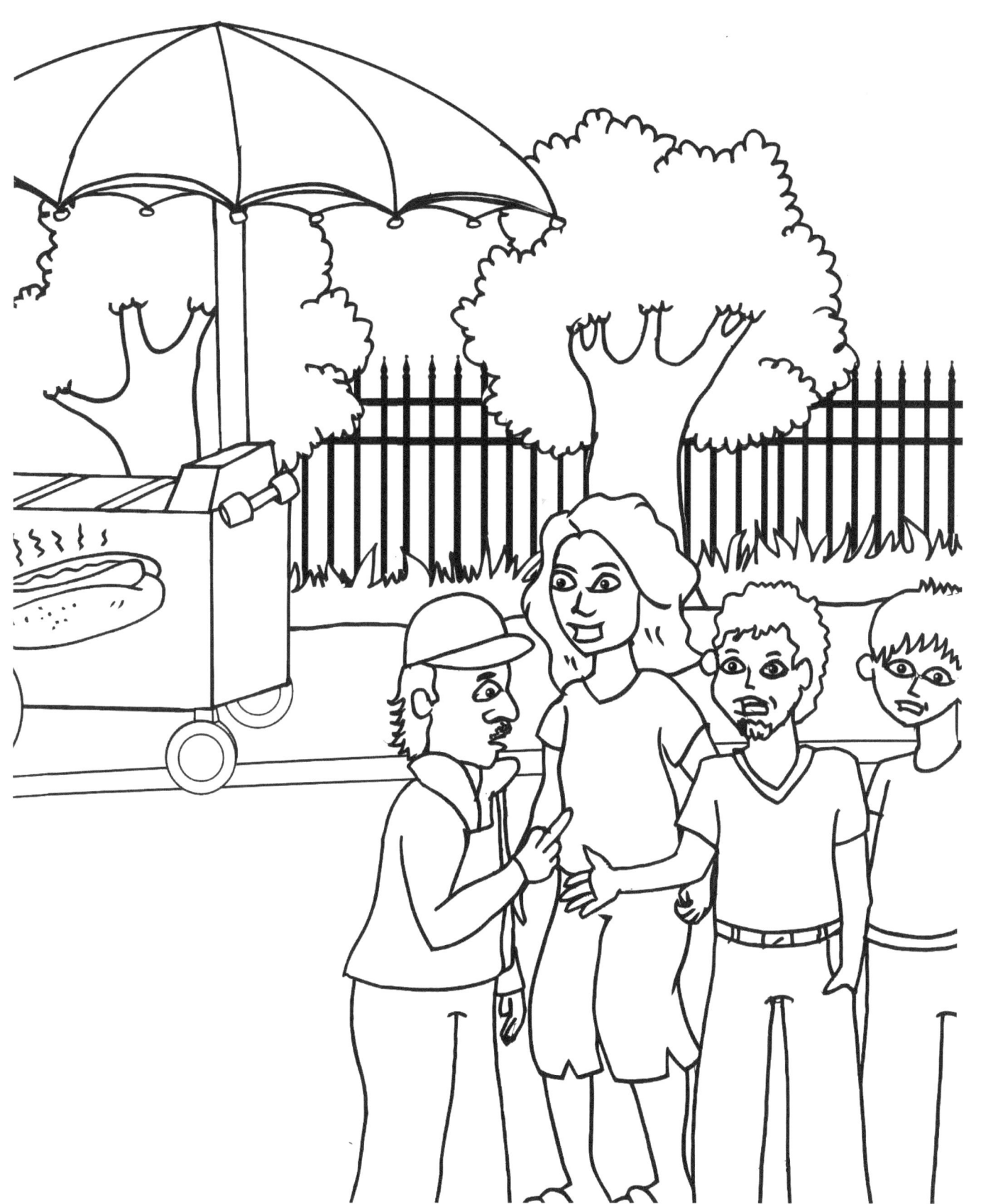

"Well, if it shouldn't eat meat why did it take the wiener from me?" the hot dog vendor asked. "That little black squirrel came right up to the fence and stretched out his tiny paws and grabbed the wiener from my hand! I didn't force it down his throat. He took it with the greatest ease. So give me a break sir, if you please!"

Pete didn't know what the hullabaloo was about. He only knew that Charlie was lying on his back on the ground, unable to stand, unable to breathe, and unable to make a sound.

Thinking quickly, Pete took off like a jet on a runway. Then he turned and sprinted back. He jumped on Charlie's chest! Pete spring boarded and landed onto the freshly mowed grass. It was his best leap ever!

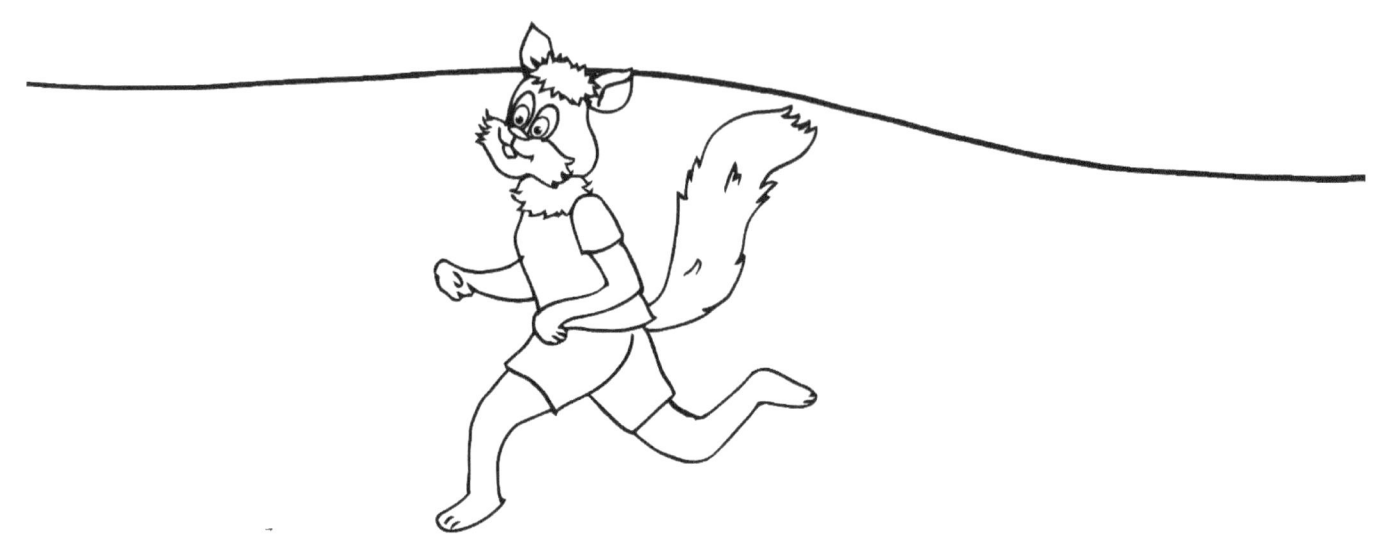

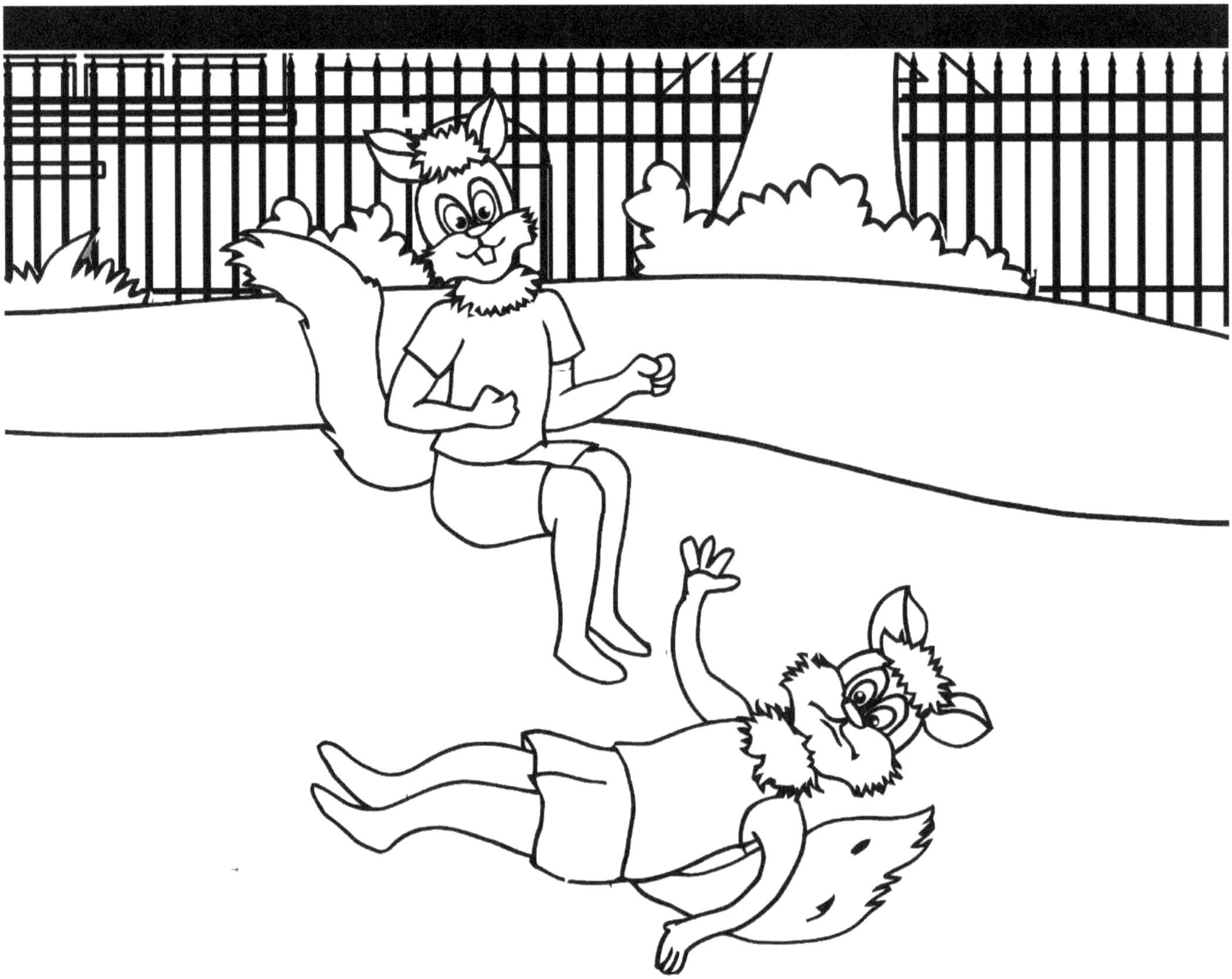

The force of the jump on Charlie's puffed up chest gave him wind, and the wiener in his throat flew like an arrow from a bow and landed on the ground with a PLOP!

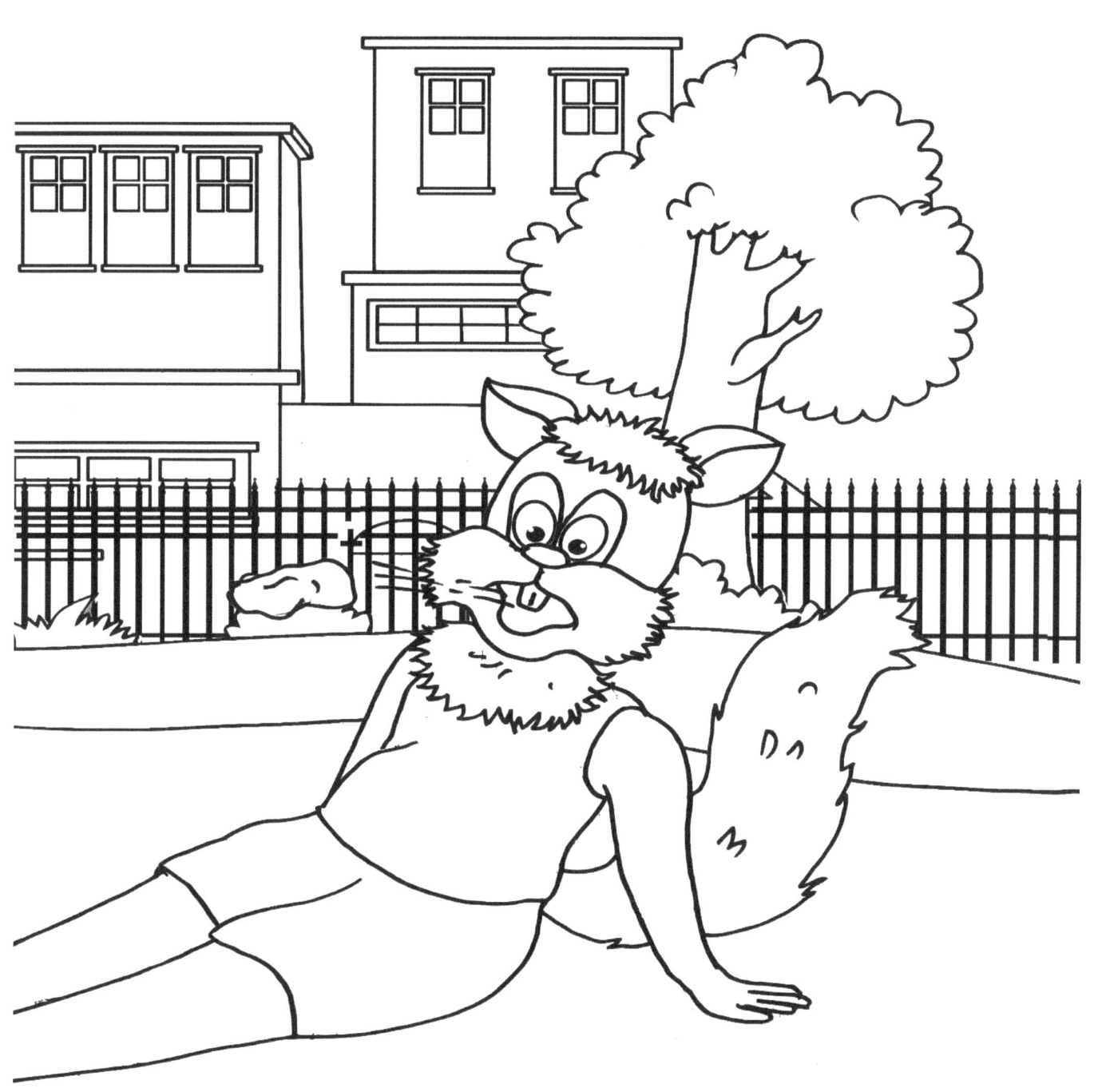

Charlie stood up on wobbly feet. His eyes returned to their normal size. The crowd cheered and applauded as if it was a grand performance.

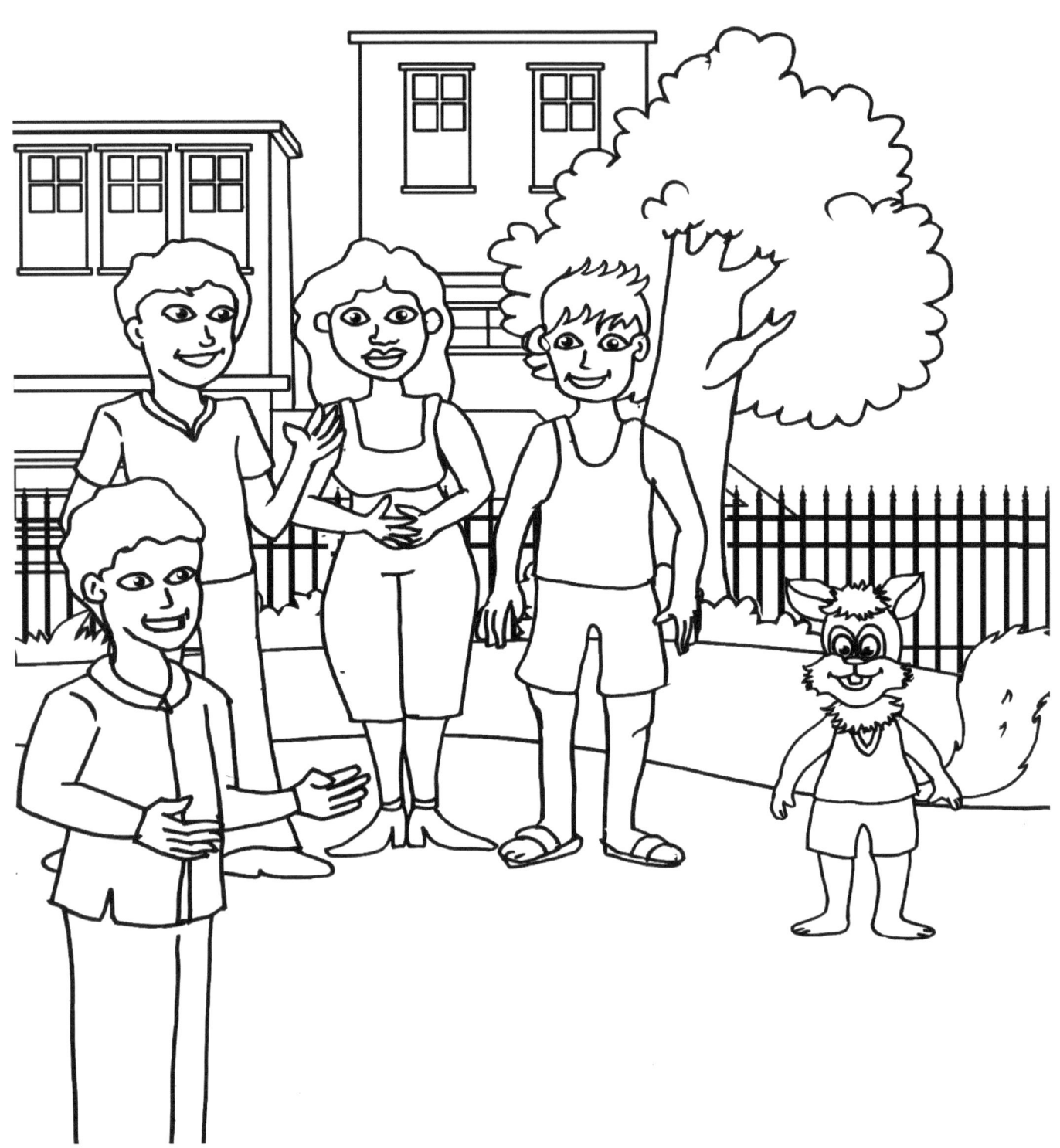

"Oh Pete, I'm sorry to cause you so much trouble. I won't do it again," Charlie said. "I know now that I should never eat meat even if someone tempts me."

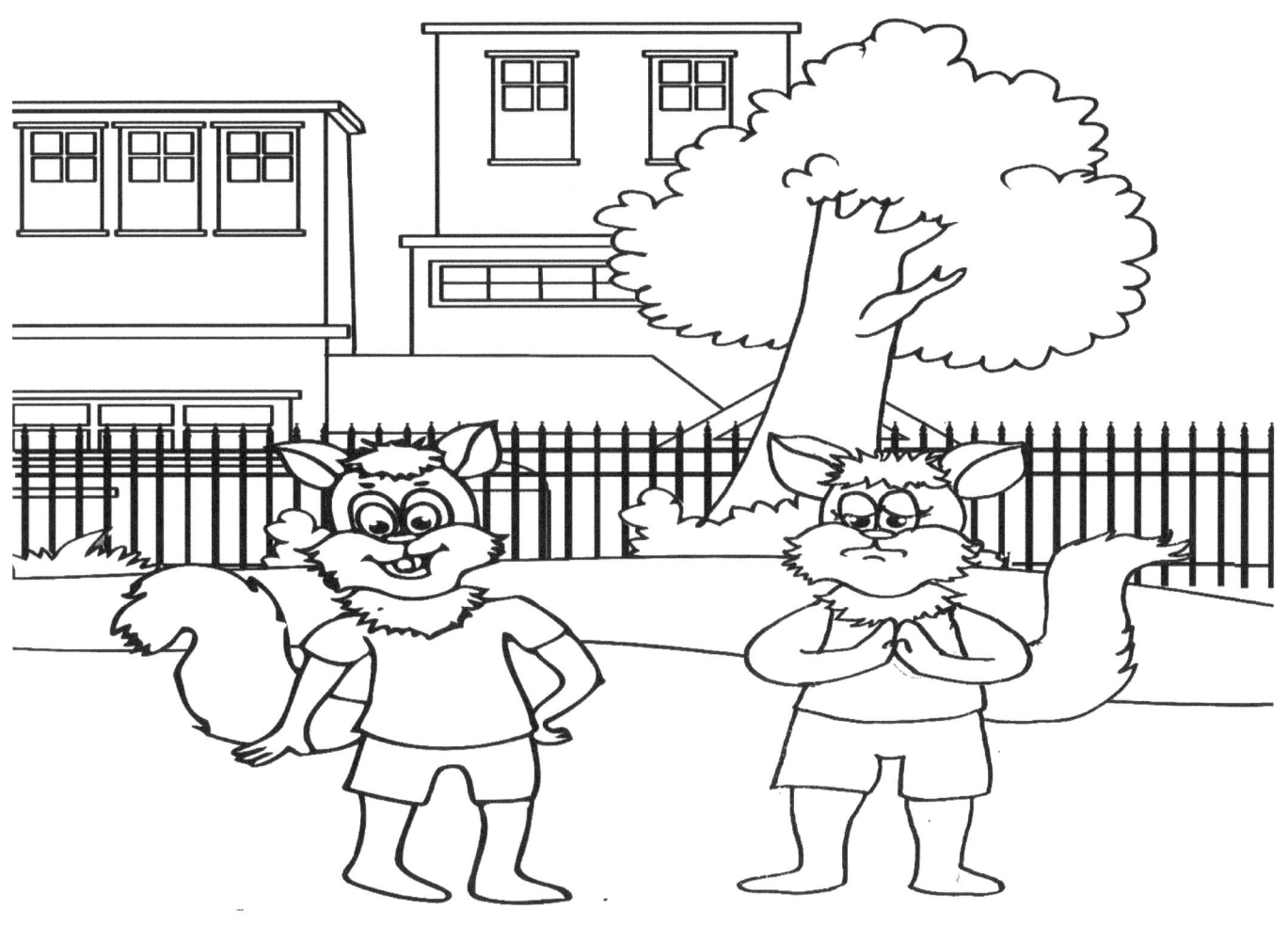

But Pete just shook his head from side to side. He knew that soon Charlie would be up to his eyeballs in another escapade. He hoped everything would end well and that he would not feel so scared again.

"You know something, Charlie? I could bet you three times . . . maybe twelve times, that you'll be in trouble again before summer ends."

"Oh no, Pete, I'm really going to try to be good."

"I think you can't help it. From now on, I'll call you Charlie Double Trouble Berryhill!"

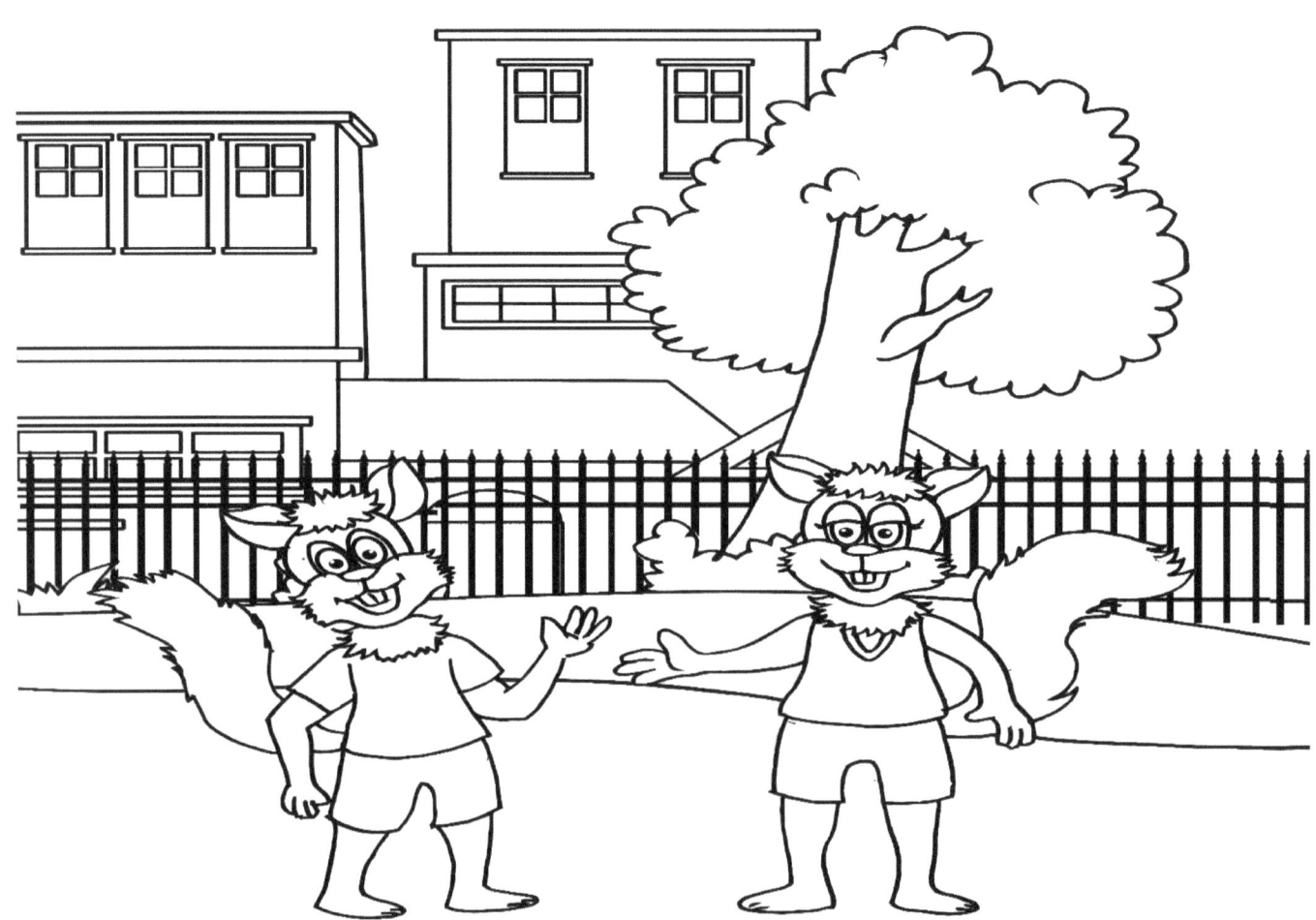

The two squirrels hugged, then strolled back to the den. They were happy to be cousins and most of all, good friends.

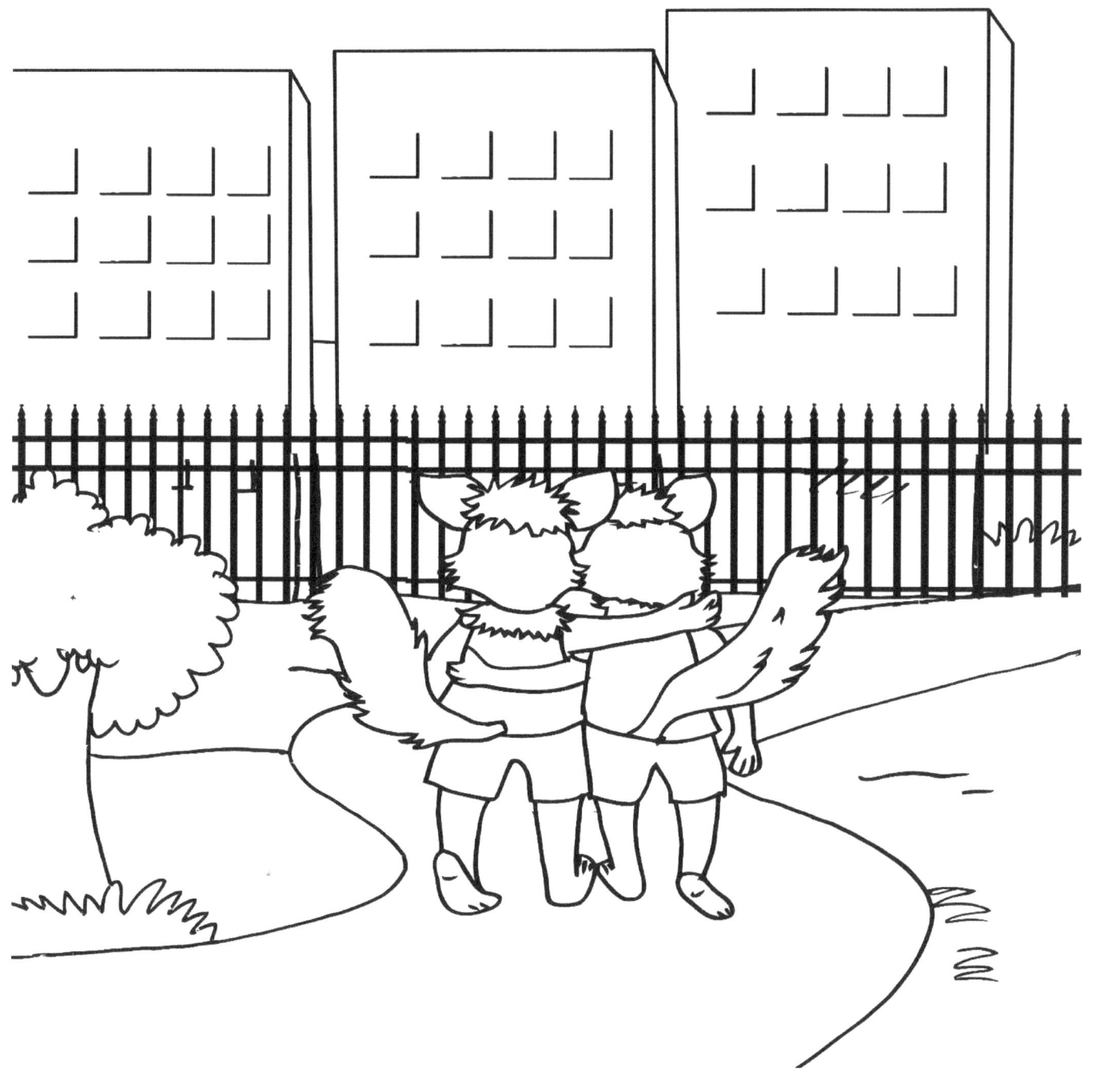

THE END

www.ingramcontent.com/pod-product-compliance
Lightning Source LLC
Chambersburg PA
CBHW041936240526
45473CB00034B/1750